GROWING ME
- The Basics -

A Workbook For Meaningful Living

Séamus Scanlan

Also by the author:

Aiming For The Pinnacle -
Coaching & Living for Self-Actualization.
LOGOSE® Publishing (2007)

Private

This book belongs to:

Contact at:

This Workthrough Commenced:

Workthrough Number:*

*You may decide to re-do this workbook in the future.

Published by: Createspace^{tm}

© Copyright 2008 Séamus Scanlan.

All rights reserved. No part of this publication may be reproduced or distributed in any form or by any means or stored in a database or retrieval system, without the prior written permission of the publisher.

ISBN: 1440402329 / 9781440402326
Edition 1.0
August 2008

To Liam & David...

Contents

	Introduction	9
1.	Get Growing.	17
2.	Limber Up.	29
3.	Take Ownership.	40
4.	Get a Service.	59
5.	Dream On…	72
6.	Aim Well.	90
7.	Review.	104

Introduction.

Let me guess.
You want to be happy. Me too!
Let me guess again.
You don't like suffering. Me too!

Let me guess once again. Some of your past decisions could have been better – to put it mildly. Guess what - me too!

Well, welcome to life - the default version of life we all get! It is as if we all get a deck of cards to play with and someone, somewhere, says 'Let's see what you do with these.'

Some of us seem to have it easier than others. Some others' grass genuinely seems to be greener. And then we get close to that grass and we discover that it *is* damn well greener than ours and more luscious, and with a breathtaking view to boot!

'Life is so unfair!' we think, as we lick our wounds – those we now decide to have from this experience. We discover that it is possible for someone to have something we would really like but *we don't have it!*

Having licked those wounds, you might then set out to better yourself. You read a few self-help books. One tells you to look inside for the reason that you don't currently feel love for your spouse. *'It's not about them but about you,'* they claim authoritatively. Another self-help book tells you to move on and get out of an unhappy relationship. Which approach should you take? Another expert tells you that you need to find the answers to *these* questions within yourself. Aaaaagh – where to turn!

Many people are avid self-help book readers. Others are truly skeptical about the whole thing – seeing it as an industry feeding off people's unhappiness. They see it as a pyramid selling scheme where a small number of people make money selling hope to a lot of others in packaging lacking a best-before date. The good feeling doesn't last for some reason.

I have to admit, for reasons related to both my work and my personal challenges, I regularly find myself in each of the two camps. I treasure a good life-enhancing book one month and I reek with skepticism another month when I encounter something quite different but which is sold under the same broad heading – 'self-help.'

Sometimes I find a book that has a small number of useful insights buried alongside some questionable propositions and/or embedded in a lot of superfluous words. With these, I simply aim to discern and escape with something of value.

I have, over the last decade, had the privilege of working alongside many people actively committed to bettering themselves in meaningful ways. I've learned so much from them - something for which I am eternally grateful. In that work, I have come to see certain patterns in both what the self-help industry offers and how its consumers respond to those offerings. Many times I get insights into outcomes ensuing from these responses. Some happy stories, some not so happy.

This book is intended to be a compact distillation of some of the insights that have shown themselves to me over those years of journeying with fellow pilgrims. Any one chapter might offer value as a stand alone statement. Taking them together, in order, is probably the most effective way to use the book.

Throughout the book are opportunities for note-taking. I strongly encourage you to write your own personal notes in these pages. Much of the value of self-help offerings come from wrestling with the subjects and finding one's own position and language out of that process.

There is another reason that your note-taking can be of huge value. It is that, in re-visiting yourself at a later date by re-reading this material and noting what you were writing in response, all those days, weeks, months or years ago, it can offer you a key benefit of making use of self-help material - that is the increasing freedom to discover, and accept, that our previous take on something was just that - ours. It was our subjective take at the time based more on what we wanted to interpret than on an objective analysis of the words on a page. We focused on certain things and glossed over others – that was then and this is now – wow!

Each of the following chapters deals with ideas that I hope are presented in succinct, accessible, sensible and practical ways. Each of the headings can be drilled into in deeper ways at a later date. The idea is to get the basics right. Get familiar with the ideas first – then consider deepening your understanding later. Even the more seasoned of us can go back to basics, with new eyes, and be all the better for it.

Séamus Scanlan
Kildare,
Ireland.
2008

Growing Me – The Basics

1. Get Growing.

The single most influential factor on the success or otherwise of a person's approach to self-help will be their understanding of personal growth.

Whoever you are, whatever age you are, you will have reached this stage of your life through the use of a range of resources and behaviors. Some of those resources will have presented themselves to you irrespective of your actions – let's call it luck for the time being. Some of those resources will have become available through your actions. Of those actions, some were thought out and some were without any particular conscious action on your part. The fact that you are reading these words indicates that you have come this far. You have been eating and drinking. Somewhere along the line you did all that was needed to learn to read – and had the opportunity to do so. You might have been a model student. You might have been a 'difficult' student, but you learned. Right now, you might be sitting in your comfortable house on your couch or in circumstances less luxurious. But you are reading – even if you are not sure why.

What we employ as we progress through our life, however wonderful or woeful we find that life to be, are our dependences. (Clarification: A 'dependency' is a word used to refer to a territory that is 'owned' by another state. It is also used sometimes in reference to a pattern of behaviors as in 'co-dependency'. Your *dependent* is someone who has a *dependence* on you).

So what is personal growth in this context?

Personal growth is the process by which we change our dependences *in a certain way*. The last bit is very important. If I am dependent on alcohol and I stop using it but start using cocaine instead, it is not growth. If I am dependent on alcohol and manage to replace this dependence with fruit juice, this may well be growth – juice is the new dependence.

Another example: John aims to achieve promotion in work every one to two years. He always has the next promotion fixed in his mind and works towards it. His wife, Mary, has been complaining that she and the kids hardly ever see him and would be quite happy for them all to take a reduction in financial standard of living if they could have regular family and spousal time together – particularly while the kids are young. John found this a huge challenge but, within about eighteen months, he had found a way to balance up his work hours and his home hours. He lost some sleep at times, he argued with Mary on occasion. It wasn't easy. He had to let go of his dependence on feeling 'top-dog' and having more than enough money to spend. In the past, every time he felt disheartened about anything, he perked himself up by focusing on achieving the next promotion or he went out and bought himself a new toy. Now, he could no longer employ these activities but had discovered something important – his family and how to live with them.

Whilst John and Mary still had, by their own admission, lots to improve on in terms of their relationship with each other and with the kids, they felt they were moving towards something better and were glad of this albeit challenging change. This was growth. John and Mary, in some subtle ways, had replaced a number of dependences with other 'better' dependences.

The move towards these new dependences seemed to achieve a by-product that both John and Mary valued as they discovered it. That by-product is *meaning* – and it made all the difference.

Understanding personal growth – what it is and isn't – can form a solid basis for any life. The beauty of it is that there is no recommended starting point – other then where you are right now. Here's a really interesting thing about it – if you want it to, your personal growth can continue right to the moment of your death. The by-products of personal growth are things like meaning, strength (through humility for example), peace or some other experiences that lift us out of where we didn't even realize we were, to somewhere we find to be compellingly, and sustainably, 'a better place'. This may entail huge changes around us or may mean simply discovering a new way of seeing things. This then leads to new perspectives without much change in those actual things. But we didn't will ourselves into these new ways of seeing things – we *grew* into them. Self-help tips that rely on will alone will not generate growth and its rewards.

Growth vs. Development.

A key feature of personal growth is that it is not the same as personal development. At least, there is value in not confusing the two.

I use the term personal development to refer to the process of acquiring new abilities. Learning to play the violin could be personal development for me. Giving up pressuring my child to pump in so many hours of violin practice may be growth for me. I might 'grow into' letting go of my need to show the world how wonderful I am (through my children) and show my children how wonderful I am by actually playing silly childish games with them.

Learning to be assertive might be personal development for one person. Learning not to use assertive behavior, when listening might be more appropriate, could be considered growth.

Context is Everything.
People often turn to self-help books when they are unhappy. Very often, we want a quick fix. We want some simple things to do so that the unhappiness goes away and that lots of happiness comes our way. Over time, we discover that

sometimes we can apply those simple habits of effectiveness and sometimes we can't. Even when we do apply them, we don't always get the results we wanted. Or, we apply them, get predicted results, are happy for a short while, and then find we are back to square one – we want more happiness. We seem to have used up the happiness that a new habit produces – we take it for granted perhaps. We might even get tired of it – 'I'm sick of understanding others – I wish to God they would understand me!'

All the scenarios in which we try to apply the advice we get in self-help books have their own context. Each context has a number of elements. We are not always aware of all the elements. In fact, we are rarely aware of all the elements. At different times we see different pieces of the jigsaw.

Despite these different contexts, there is a pervasive theme for all of us - our growth. Each situation, happy or unhappy, presents some little or large opportunity to look at our dependences and change them for the better. If we take advantage of them, the accumulation of these opportunities gives us the rewards of growth. Even if our outward circumstances are at times bewildering, our inner experience can be different – the better for the growth.

Just because we read self-books does not mean that we won't have to face the difficulties of life from time to time. However, with real growth, we develop real resilience. With real resilience, we are much more likely to thrive than not. This is how we get sustainable value from the process.

Let's do some exercises...

Strategy No.1 :
Understand Personal Growth and make it a central feature of your life.

Start Here:

1.1. Without going back to the text, write what you understand personal growth to be.

1.2. Now go back, examine the text, and write down what this book is suggesting personal growth to be.

1.3. List the most important dependences in your life at this time (In any order, 'good' or 'bad' for now):

1.4. Write a sentence to reflect your level of commitment to your own personal growth from here on in. (Just making the statement helps!):

1.5. Take a break:

Well done. You've done something worthwhile.

Now go off and do something different. Watch an episode of your favorite TV program, go for a walk, meet a friend for coffee (but don't overdo it if you start talking about your personal growth!)

Do something physical – get some air! Personal Growth is as much about *letting* certain things happen as it is about *making* something happen.

When you come back, look at what you have written and move on to the next chapter.

2. Limber Up.

We often look at things as if we were Einstein - as if we had figured out what was happening. Even Einstein disliked making such assumptions.

Having briefly looked at the concept of personal growth, let's look at something you are going to be using as you aim to accelerate your growth – that something is your thinking.

Whenever a person picks up and reads a self-help book (or any other book for that matter) they read the book through their own eyes. We might understand the words exactly as the writer intended (or we might not sometimes) but we interpret the implications of the words with our own 'weightings'.

Caroline read a piece of a 'laws of success' type book that suggested that, to achieve success, one needed to take responsibility. She spent that evening complaining to her current partner how 'irresponsible' men are - with regular references to her ex-husband who had left her five years previously.

Caroline understood the words of the statement in the book but moved the weightings of the implications to a personally selected target. At a later time, I will look at possible underlying reasons for Caroline's type of response but, for now, let me say that Caroline is intelligent. At a time in the future, she will reflect on 'the old her' and see that she had looked at the phrase in the success book in a certain way. On reflection, she sees that she 'needed' to interpret things a certain way. She will realize that she had a dependence on a certain cluster of beliefs that, at the time, she thought of as objective, but later saw as subjective and possibly quite irrational. With this reflection, she thinks something like: *'If only I had seen my own subjectivity, things might have been so different. I might not have been so angry and resentful all those years. All that time that could have been used for love, instead of bitterness.'*

Caroline's need to see things a certain way was effectively a dependence. The day she replaced that dependence with a more productive one (one that left more space for love, fun, intimacy, joy etc.), was the day she outgrew that dependence. This is not saying that suddenly everything in her life is as she would like it to be, but it does mean she is in a better place to appreciate what she does have without the burden of bitterness. If only there was some way to bring forward that growth – to get to it faster. I suggest there is.

One of the most pervasive conditions afflicting us as members of the human race is arrogance. I am not talking here of people who appear brash and arrogant. I am simply talking about our tendency to operate as if we have all the relevant facts. We make decisions and then claim is it because .... (we fill in the blanks). We might do this quietly and unobtrusively or we might do it with great fanfare.

The assumption that we have all the relevant facts is an example of what might be termed unhygienic thinking. If we are all like Caroline, and reflect that our decisions and our levels of meaningful happiness may depend on our ability to see things objectively, then seeing our own subjectivity might point towards opportunities for growth. The key here is to see any possible attachments to a particular truth. How do we feel when an ostensibly rational argument is presented to us that could potentially fly in the face of our current perspectives?

The notion of cleaning up ones' thinking can be quite a challenge. For thousands of years philosophers and others have tried to present alternative ways of seeing things. Does one need to become a philosopher to get the best out of life? To a degree, one might say yes to that question – hence the generous shelves in the philosophy and popular psychology sections of book-shops the world over.

I don't propose re-inventing the wheel here in terms of philosophy, but I do suggest one simple ingredient – humility. The simplest and quickest way in which we can begin to cleanse our thinking is to stop thinking that our 'reality' is reality. It is said that a mind is like a parachute – they both work best when they are open.

So how do we open our minds? This is a notoriously tricky one. As well as that, it is not even an open or shut case – more a matter of degree. If our goal is personal growth, we will be looking for ways in which our mind is relying on its current 'take'. We can interrogate our thinking – and there is value in that. However, if we have an emotional attachment to seeing things a certain way, we are likely to get stuck during this interrogation or give up prematurely. If we could find and understand our emotional attachments, we might go some of the way to freeing ourselves up for more objective thinking – a more open mind and more hygienic thinking.

In the next section, I will be looking at the area of emotions and how to get them working for us rather than against us. For the moment, I suggest a few simple exercises. Think of these in terms of the metaphor of learning to play a musical instrument. You don't start trying to play Mozart in your first lesson. What we often do is we think in terms of opening our mind to the possibility of limited thinking when someone 'proves' something to us. What I am suggesting here is simply some warming up that might help prepare for opportunities for growth when they present themselves.

For some of these exercises, you may want to seek opinions from someone who knows you.

Strategy No.2:
Prepare your mind for some new thinking.

Start Here:

2.1. Write you own personal philosophy of life! Make ten short statements that reflect your unique personal outlook on life.

a.
b.
c.
d.
e.
f.
g.
h
i.
j.

2.2. Describe a situation where someone you know behaved as if they had what you consider to be an unreasonable expectation of you.

2.3. Describe a situation where someone else seemed to suggest that you had an unreasonable expectation of them.

2.4. Describe a situation where someone you know did something stupid.

Growing Me – The Basics

2.5. Describe a situation where *you* did something you now see as stupid. Not so easy? – give it your best shot.

2.6. Describe one belief you have for which there is some conflicting evidence. E.g. we do/do not go somewhere after we die.

For the purposes of this exercise, there is no need to present arguments either way.

2.7. Take a break.

As before, take some time out now.

If you feel a bit stuck on any question don't worry. Reflect on it after you go for a walk or a cycle or a drive. Or even sleep on it. The whole idea is that you are practicing *allowing* your mind to open not trying to *force* it to open.

When you come back to the book, if necessary finish the questions as best you can and remind yourself of what you have written so far.

3. Take Ownership.

Message on a refrigerator magnet:
'I know it's not your fault,
I'm just blaming you.'

There was a time when a small number of people were ridiculed for suggesting that the Earth orbited the Sun. Times have changed – or have they?

One of the ways in which our quality of life improves is when we discover a fallacy – a lie. It might hurt when we discover someone we love has betrayed us, but other things also fall into place. *'Ah...that explains why he was going on so many business trips - he was with her - at least I know now - the suspicion was driving me insane – the bastard!'*

When we discover a truth, we might not like it but once we accept it, we can make informed decisions – sometimes very difficult . Perhaps for a while we wish we had never found out but we can't put it back in the box.

When early astronomers, many years ago, tried to make sense of the skies, they used mathematical calculations to predict the movement of stars and planets. No amount of bending the figures would allow them to accurately predict the position of heavenly bodies if they did not have the basic structure right. Eventually, courageous astronomers confronted the status quo. Now we take the fact that the Earth travels round the sun as just that – fact. And with that fact, astronaut navigators can plot courses for satellites, probes and shuttles with predictable accuracy – it works.

But, there was a time when large numbers of educated people not only *believed* that the Earth orbited the Sun but they *wanted* it to be true! Why, in God's name, would anyone have an emotional attachment to such an astronomical theory? Either way, the sun continued to shine, day and night, came and went, and the seasons did what they had done for a long long time. None of this changed because a new understanding of the solar system was finally accepted. The reason was that somewhere in the lives of the people who wanted to believe the old way, were dependences that were not shed easily. I don't propose to go into detail here on what those dependences were but I do want to highlight that such dependences can exist.

As I have alluded to before, the work I have done over the years, alongside countless individuals who committed themselves to bettering themselves, has revealed a number of insights. One of those has been about personal growth. Another has been about hygienic thinking. However, the insight that represents the most powerful challenge for any of us relates to how we understand our emotions.

There is an assumption deeply embedded in the minds of the vast majority of the members of the human race. That assumption is that it is external events that cause negative emotions. And as negative emotions are what get in the way of my happiness or success, then it must be external events that are the cause of my unhappiness and lack of progress. But that pervasive assumption is flawed. It is not external events that cause our negative emotions, it is us – it is the way we interpret the events.

If I was asked to pick out one self-help tip that had the most potential to transform a person's life for the better, I would suggest what I call 'Emotional Ownership'.

When someone insults me I feel something. If someone says something to you like *'You're such a selfish schmuck!'* , how do you feel? In the vast majority of cases, you will experience a feeling that you wouldn't particularly go out of your way to achieve. You would like it to go away. If you felt affirmed and complemented, you would want to wallow in it a little – take the credit. If someone insults you, you are unlikely to ask them to keep saying it to you. Such are negative emotions.

Okay, let's give you the benefit of the doubt and say that of course you're not a selfish schmuck but you still feel the hit when someone throws this at you.

Emotional ownership is about noticing those feelings, noticing your inner responses, mental and emotional, to the words that have just been fired at you. It then involves allowing those feelings to work their way through you until they settle and dissipate – without yet trying to prove to yourself, or someone else, that they are wrong in their criticism of you. Then, when the wave of emotion has washed its way through you, you decide how you want to respond to the situation.

This washing through process is based on the idea that the negative emotions are the product of the gap between our expectations and what is happening. By allowing that gap to be noticed and allowing our expectation to accept that they were not met, something subtle happens within us. Something is changed. We change.

Of course we could rally the troops, inner and outer. We could latch on to evidence that we are not what our insulter accuses us of. We might list, to ourselves, times in the past when we were so generous. We turn to friends and loved ones for them to confirm to us that we are okay – and the feeling gets relieved.

In the first case, we let the feelings wash through us and something happened. We allowed ourselves to feel all that went with the insult and we came through the other side. In the second case we didn't go through it – we closed the door and retained our perception of ourselves – the one we are currently dependent on. We missed an opportunity for growth - we might even have had to revise our idea of a selfish schmuck – we might have opened our mind!

In the self-help field we sometimes hear two different schools of thought that might seem contradictory.

School 1: The Positive Thinking School.
School 2: The Face Your Demons School.

The first school suggests that we just concentrate on our future goals, avoid any negative thoughts or feelings (or even people) and stay focused on what we want.

The second school says that if you don't face your demons (negative emotions) you will never be free to get the best out of your life.

I propose a third school. The 'Make a Distinction' School. This is based on the idea that there are two types of negative emotions as follows:

1. Existential Negative Emotions.
2. Neurotic Negative Emotions.

The first lot of emotions are the ones we must face – that we must resolve and generally give up trying to relieve. The second are the ones we generate ourselves and can stop generating if we apply ourselves. In fact, the resolution of the existential emotions leaves us in a better position to stop generating the neurotic emotions. Willing ourselves to get rid of either is like trying to teach a cat to play the saxophone – it consumes a lot of energy, it doesn't work and it annoys the cat – who has better things to be doing!

In very brief terms, examples of existential feelings are:

Grief: I am letting go of something.

Remorse: I am accepting responsibility.

Hurt: I am acknowledging the reality of a betrayal.

Examples of neurotic emotions might be:

Guilt: I keep going over it over and over again.

Anger: I make myself angry to avoid hurt.

Bitterness: Until I finally grieve.

I accept that this seems a very simplistic approach to the complicated business of emotions, but I urge the reader to reflect on it and observe yourself and those around you. Have you ever witnessed a genuine episode of remorse? Have you ever noticed how someone keeps talking over and over about something 'bad' they did – how guilty they feel?

One last thing about emotions - they can be elusive. Just because I don't consciously feel something doesn't mean that the feeling isn't there somewhere in the background. Feelings are an awareness thing. By the same token, just because you notice one feeling, it doesn't mean that you're aware of *all* your feelings. Feelings hide because of their implications for dependences. If I see myself as a victim (a dependence), it might be easy to allow myself to feel hurt – but I might not feel remorse so easily. I might feel compassion for one person but disdain for another in a similar situation.

This book is designed to be an accessible short read. The area of emotions and the psychology around them is an area for huge discussion and debate. The reader is advised to tread softly –

when it comes to your own emotions and those of others.

Time for some exercises.

Strategy No.3 :
Prepare to start taking emotional ownership.

Start Here:

3.1. List your fears – what are the five things that frighten you most – apart from death.
a
b
c
d
e

Growing Me – The Basics

3.2. Take each one of your answers at Question 1 and list the worst thing that could happen in each case.

a
b
c
d
e

3.3. Take each one of your answers at Question 2 and estimate the likelihood of these things happening.

a
b
c
d
e

3.4. Take each one of your answers and state what you would do after the feared event if it did happen.

a

b

c

d

e

3.5. List the five scariest things you have ever done.

a

b

c

d

e

Growing Me – The Basics

3.6. If you were to do these again, do you believe each would be less scary, more scary, or the same.

a

b

c

d

e

3.7. List five new things you would find scary to do but you think might benefit you.

a

b

c

d

e

3.8. Of the things you listed at questions 7, what would be the benefits of doing each?

a

b

c

d

e

3.9. Of the things you listed at question 7, how prepared are you to do them now?

a

b

c

d

e

3.10. List the people who most make you experience negative emotions and the predominant feeling in each case.

a

b

c

d

e

3.11. If you were not negatively affected by those feelings, how would you describe those relationships?

a

b

c

d

e

3.12. To what degree do you believe you create your own negative emotions in the case of each of these people and why?

a _____

b _____

c _____

d _____

e _____

Time to take break!

If you have completed all those questions, you may well find your mind churned up. Now is the time to play again. Don't be surprised if you feel somewhat confused. When it comes to moving towards emotional ownership, confusion is very common. With patience however, the mist will dissipate and a clearer sense of direction will appear.

As you play, or especially as you interact with others, observe your inner responses to events and words. Just take note mentally and when you return to the book jot, down your initial observations and how they might be relevant to the concept of emotional ownership.

4. Get A Service.

Mens sana in corpore sano
(Latin: A healthy mind in a healthy body.)

I once spoke with a medical doctor and we found ourselves on the subject of complementary health. He did not seem favorably disposed to the industry. I pointed out to him that it is an industry and that therefore a lot of people were choosing to avail of its products and services. I asked if he thought that they were misguided. He changed the subject.

A key feature of the complementary approach to healthcare is the notion of 'holism' – it is holistic in its approach. This is sometimes referred to as a body-mind approach or a body-mind-spirit approach. Conventional western medicine has emphasized a scientific approach to the use of any procedure or substance in the treatment of disease. Frequently, that conventional body of wisdom claims that the complementary health field is not scientific enough. However, the complementary health industry continues to grow and I for one keep hearing first hand stories of satisfied customers. I also hear of 'no result' stories - the type of which I have also often heard, and indeed take for granted, from the conventional side of the fence. Neither side is without the odd 'horror story'.

I try to avoid taking sides in this healthcare dichotomy and remain interested in what each side has to offer. The key piece of the equation is this: everyone wants happiness (in whatever form that might take for any one of us at any time). Happiness is a state of mind. Your state of mind is influenced by at least two things:

1. Your experiences.
2. Your physiology.

There may be other influencers, but I am sticking to these because I have found that we can exercise some influence over them.

Much of the rest of this book is about our experiences and what we do in response to them. This chapter is about our physiology.

Have you ever found yourself tired and irritable? I guess you have. What is happening at those times? You are less patient with other people. Things that don't normally bother you really annoy you. The things and people are more or less the same but you are responding to them differently. The next day you might see things with fresh eyes.

Did you ever meet someone who is difficult to be with when they are hungry? Not uncommon in small children – tired and hungry and quick to try our patience! The fact is that our state of mind is influenced by our physiology. And, of course, the reverse applies: our physiology is influenced by our state of mind. Are you not in a different state of mind when you have had a few too many glasses of alcohol? Do you not feel off when you experience a big disappointment?

This is not designed to be a reference book and the ideas presented are limited to those that can be tested in a short space of time by anyone. In other words, I do not propose trying to convince any reader of the truth of anything by reference to a series of 'double-blind controlled' studies that have been put forward for peer review. Our state of mind is influenced by our physiology and if we want to aim for higher levels of meaningful existence, we need to keep that in mind.

So what can we do to help our state of mind from a physiological perspective? Try these five ways:

1. Improve the quality of our diet.
2. Ensure that we do enough of the right exercise.
3. Reduce our consumption of toxins.
4. Identify, and act on, any allergies we have.
5. Support our body's excretory systems.

Exactly how you apply yourself to these five objectives will depend on your own needs and circumstances. It will also depend on your state of mind! Yes, there is a circular relationship. How you apply yourself to your own self-care will be effected by your state of mind and your state of mind will be effected, amongst others things, by your level of self-care. One helps the other – not one or the other – both.

When it comes to physiological self-care, there seems to be a lot of expertise out there. This book is offered at an 'executive' level (not in the business sense but in the sense of exercising executive control over one's life) and will deliberately not be suggesting the minutia of how to apply oneself to the five objectives above.

I will stress however, that if you are currently neglecting your physiological self-care, that whatever level of success or life-productivity you are achieving now, it a safe bet that it would be better if you improved your self-care. Of course, when I talk about improving our self-care, I am not talking about an obsessional approach that looses sight of other aspects of our life. I am talking about a measured, grounded approach - possibly a 'small step at a time' approach - but one that takes us in the right direction.

In summary, if you want to build a life characterized by meaningful engagement, you need to give yourself a service and develop a strategy for continually improving physiological self-care.

Time for some exercises....

Strategy No.4 :
Develop a strategy for continually improving physiological self-care.

Start Here:

4.1. Research high quality diet/eating habits.

Number of hours research I will do: ☐
I will do this research by this date : ☐
My results will be in the following format:
☐

I completed this task on this date: ☐

Or

I am deciding not to invest time in this area.
I accept the possible trade-offs for this.

Date this decision is being made: ☐

4.2. Quality Diet Action:
Based on my research, I will do:
Tip: Use bite-size tasks.
If nothing write 'Nothing' and the dates.

#	Target Date	Action	Completion Date

Strategy No.4 : Continued.
Develop a strategy for continually improving physiological self-care.

4.3. Research the role of effective exercise.

Number of hours research I will do: ☐
I will do this research by this date: ☐

My results will be in the following format:
☐

I completed this task on this date: ☐

Or

I am deciding not to invest time in this area.
I accept the possible trade-offs for this.

Date this decision is being made: ☐

4.4. Effective Exercise Action:
Based on my research I will do the following.
Tip: Use bite-size tasks.
If nothing write 'Nothing' and the dates.

#	Target Date	Action	Completion Date

Strategy No.4 : Continued.
Develop a strategy for continually improving physiological self-care.

4.5. Research the role of toxins in well-being.

Number of hours research I will do: ☐
I will do this research by this date: ☐

My results will be in the following format:
☐

I completed this task on this date: ☐

Or

I am deciding not to invest time in this area.
I accept the possible trade-offs for this.

Date this decision is being made: ☐

4.6. Toxins Action:
Based on my research I will do the following.
Tip: Use bite-size tasks.
If nothing write 'Nothing' and the dates.

#	Target Date	Action	Completion Date

5. Dream On...

When you are dragged down by your obstacles, allow yourself to be lifted up by your dreams.

One of the most useful and, in my opinion, one of the most underused questions available to all of us is: 'What do you want?' or 'What do I want?'

Much of what we achieve or experience in life is influenced by how and what we want. 'How does *how we want* make sense?' you might ask. 'Surely you want or you don't want and it is as simple as that.' If you stop and think about it, you will find that there is more to it.

Have you ever heard someone talk about something they say they want but you notice that they never seem to be doing anything about achieving it? That is one type of wanting. Have you ever seen someone do things that are designed to get them to something they want? They quietly, or noisily, apply themselves to a series of tasks, some easy some hard, that inch them towards this objective of theirs. They sometimes fail in these tasks but they still persevere. Isn't that a different type of wanting to the first type?

Do you ever daydream? If not, I recommend it. Oscar Wilde, the Irish writer, is quoted as having said : *"A dreamer is one who can only find his way by moonlight, and his punishment is that he sees the dawn before the rest of the world."* Yes, we can stick our head in the sand and dream away until life bites us on the butt. We can also allocate time to quality dreaming without neglecting our responsibilities.

In aiming for a meaningful life we will need access to more than the surface layers of our heart. We'll have to go deeper and one of the ways of mining these depths is through our day-dreams. You will have guessed that I am not talking here of the sleep type of dreaming. When it comes to sleep dreams there are many opinions as to what they are, and what they do, but this is a separate issue. No, the dreams I am talking about here are the potential futures we create in our minds, complete with accompanying emotions – subtle or otherwise. They are those little video clips that float around in our consciousness depicting an alternative to our current reality. In some ways, we can be slightly inebriated by our dreams. We sigh. We play with the pictures. We deliberately plant things, people and places into the dream or these somehow seem to find their way in without us consciously prompting them. And how do we feel when we are being pampered by such dreams? When we see ourselves doing a lot of lovely things that we're not doing now? The words *'If only'* seem to sneak out under the cover of the next sigh.

But what also happens? A little voice is whispering in the background: *'Not a chance'* or *'No way'* or *'Dream on'.* No sooner have we been bathing ourselves in a wishful fantasy, then we pull the plug and let all that amniotic fluid down the drain.

What if we went a little further than we usually go? What if we accepted that we were playing with a dream and that, in the playing, we get to gradually detect snippets of a new reality – one that is available to us even if we can't quite predict all of its qualities in high definition crystal clear pictures? What if we had a habit of pulling the plug a little too early — like turning off a story before its full message could be revealed.

One of the most common pitfalls I believe people encounter when aiming for a new life, is that they do not do enough quality dreaming. They may be great at goal-setting, which we'll cover in the next chapter, but because they have not done enough rummaging into the depths of their heart, their goal-setting will be less than productive — it might even be disheartening down the road.

'But I could never have that?' This is a common response to a wonderful fantastic dream. I suggest asking yourself the following questions.
1. How much of it could I have?
2. Can I act as if I could have more than that?
3. Could I (little ol' me) grow into it gradually?
4. Could I embrace meaningful growth?

We often confuse dreaming with goal-setting or start goal-setting before the dreaming is done. We kill off one process before it has a chance to do its work by sweeping it aside to make room for another.

Let's say John is a really good driver. He takes pride in his car and he handles the machine with precision and skill. He's good at seeing potential hazards well in advance. He indicates every time and knows the meaning of all the traffic signs. He keeps his car in pristine condition – serviced at the correct intervals, washed every week and the interior is immaculate. John's way of looking after his car says nothing about his sense of direction however! He could be regularly getting lost or ending up in the wrong place. He might have gotten there without a hitch and the car might be in perfect condition when he gets there but 'there' is not where he wanted to be! Such is the relationship between our dreaming and our goal-setting.

Can you invest in some quality dreaming? Can you afford to? Can you afford not to? Here's a tip: Allocate at least 20 minutes per day to active dreaming unless your days are too crammed in which case you need to allocate three times that!

Strategy No.5 : Learn to do some dreaming.

Start Here:

5.1. Prepare for dreaming.
Familiarize yourself with the tips on the next page. Then write out each one on the facing page and tick the box when done. This actually helps to prepare you.

Don't start dreaming yet!

	Prepare for dreaming.
1	Get a pen and paper.
2	Decide time – when you won't be disturbed.
3	Date: Time:
4	Decide on a place:
5	Decide duration (30 mins? all morning?):
6	How will you know the time is up?
7	What background sounds - if any ?
8	
9	Do you want to record your spoken words?
10	How?
11	Aim to note each thought/sound.
12	And let it float in your mind or fade away.
13	Continue with this for a few minutes.
14	Bring one desire into your thoughts.
15	Allow it to float with other thoughts.
16	Note how the thoughts interact.
17	When you notice something you like say:
18	Hmmm….yes please.
19	When you notice something unwanted say:
20	Hmmm… no thanks!
21	Add other desires to taste.
22	Are you ready to do bit of free dreaming?
23	Transcribe this page onto the next page.

Growing Me – The Basics

✓	**Prepare for dreaming.**
1	
2	
3	
4	
5	
6	
7	
8	
9	
10	
11	
12	
13	
14	
15	
16	
17	
18	
19	
20	
21	
22	
23	

5.2. Start an initial list of your desires.
Don't go onto the next question until you have done this list.

And don't start dreaming yet!

1	
2	
3	
4	
5	
6	
7	
8	
9	
10	
11	
12	
13	
14	

Growing Me – The Basics

15	
16	
17	
18	
19	
20	
21	
22	
23	
24	
25	
26	
27	
28	
29	
30	
31	

5.3. Take some prompts: Go through this list and see if it prompts you to add any more desires to your list in the previous exercise.

1	Be happy
2	Feel loved
3	Have more fun
4	Visit a country
5	Learn a language
6	Learn to play a musical instrument
7	Get your voice trained
8	Learn to dance
9	Go back to college
10	Set up a charity organization
11	Go on a trek
12	Write a book
13	Have a family
14	Move house

15	Pay off your debts
16	Get a dream car/yacht/house/airplane
17	Be beaming from health & fitness
18	Be much more confident
19	Be much more humble
20	Lighten up
21	Get more grounded
22	Join/leave a specific organization
23	Make up with someone
24	Start playing a sport
25	Give up a bad habit
26	Start a new good habit
27	Die content
28	Love more
29	Be more courageous
30	Be more socially aware
31	Do a parachute jump

5.4. Write your epitaph!

Write out what you would like to have said about you after you die. (And what you would like on your gravestone!)

Growing Me – The Basics

5.5. Dream!

Review your answers to previous questions in this chapter and go ahead and dream. Don't go on to the next chapter until you have done at least three sessions.

Take notes on what you noticed at each session. Highlight repeat patterns.

Session 1 Date:	Notes
Session 2 Date:	Notes

Growing Me – The Basics

Session 3 Date:	Notes
Session 4 Date:	Notes
Session 5 Date:	Notes

Séamus Scanlan

6. Aim Well.

The one thing a dream has that a goal has not - is that it doesn't need to be measured.
One thing that a goal has that a dream has not - is a deadline!

The process of aiming well is about effective goal-setting. A dream is free to do whatever it wants — this is in the nature of dreams. A goal on the other hand has to be accountable to reality if it is to be true to its nature.

Let your goals be MAP'D!

Measurable
Attractive
Possible
Deadlined

Have a look at the following desires and mark which ones you think are measurable, attractive, possible or deadlined. In the columns, mark M, A, P, or D if applicable. Leave blank if not.

#	Desire	M	A	P	D
1	Drive a motor-home through Europe.				
2	Fly him/her to the moon and back tonight!				
3	Make my own wedding dress by next Christmas.				
4	Make more money and spend it wisely.				
5	Run in a charity mini-marathon before next July.				
6	Eat less fast food for the next three months.				
7	Love her/him madly for the rest of my life.				
8	Make love with him/her twice a week and more on vacation.				
9	Do all the exercises in this book, with a pen, before this date:_____				

Growing Me – The Basics

10	Forgive him/her/them from this moment on.				
11	Loose weight by my next birthday.				
12	Write a book by the end of next year.				
13	Write it to at least 250 pages and get 10 honest reviews.				
14	Win the lottery and buy a house for each of my friends.				
15	Make a record of every time I loose my temper over 12 months.				

Okay. Let's see what way we each marked them:

#	Desire	M	A	P	D
1	Drive a motor-home through Europe.	M	A	P	
2	Fly him/her to the moon and back tonight!	M	A		D

3	Make my own wedding dress by next Christmas.	M		P	D
4	Make more money and spend it wisely.	m	A	P	
5	Run in a charity mini-marathon before next July.	M	A	P	D
6	Eat less fast food for the next three months.	m	a	P	D
7	Love her/him madly for the rest of my life.	M ?	A	P ?	D
8	Make love with him/her twice a week and more on vacation.	M	A	P	D
9	Do all the exercises in this book, with a pen, before this date: _____	M	A	P	D
10	Forgive him/her/them from this moment on.	N	O	T	E
11	Loose weight by my next birthday.	m		P	D

12	Write a book by the end of next year.	m	A	P	D
13	Write it to at least 250 pages and get 10 honest reviews.	M	A	P	D
14	Win the lottery and buy a house for each of my friends.	M	A	p	D
15	Make a record of every time I loose my temper in the next 12 months.	M		P	D

Let's take a closer look at them:

#	Desire
1	**Drive a motor-home through Europe.** *This is **measurable** but we will need to decide what constitutes 'Europe'. Is it **attractive?** It is to me – I can't wait – when are we going? Is it **possible?** Yes, it is. Can't do it right now but some time. Is it **deadlined?** Nope! Nice dream!*
2	**Fly him/her to the moon and back tonight!** ***Measurable*** *no doubt. Let's agree that we have to touch the surface of the moon. Or let's make it easier – just do one orbit and*

	take in the scenery – great! Is it **attractive**? I suppose it is - I could be like Superman carrying Lois Lane through the heavens – quite romantic. Is it **deadlined**? You bet – lets' do it now. Is it **possible?** Hmm... let's leave this one for a more advanced workbook!
3	**Make my own wedding dress by next Christmas.** *Measurable?* Why not – a dress is a dress. Might want to pin it down a bit though! *Attractive* goal? Not quite for me. Don't really see myself in a wedding dress unless I become a drag artist. *Possible?* I am quite good with my hands. If I put my heart in it I probably could have a go. *Deadlined* – yep... down the catwalk by next Christmas!
4	**Make more money and spend it wisely.** *Measurable?* I put a small 'm' in this one. Yes 'more' is measurable. Even 1c more will achieve the goal. Better to specify an amount that can be counted. *Attractive?* You need to ask? *Possible?* More is very possible – I'm sure I can make 1c more. *Deadlined* – no.
5	**Run in a charity mini-marathon before next July.**

	Measurable? *I gave that a big M even though you could add in a measure of speed – i.e. what time am I aiming for.* ***Attractive?*** *Hmm... I am struggling with this one. If I set this as a goal, I could easily give up before I get there. It hasn't really featured in my dreams – yet!* ***Possible?*** *Yes – I'm reasonable fit and could train for it.* ***Deadlined?*** *Yes – by next July (might be worth specifying 1st, 31st, whatever).*
6	**Eat less fast food for the next three months.** ***Measurable?*** *Yes, but 'less' is like the 1c above. Better to give it a specific amount. However, if you aimed to eat less every month and stuck at it, the cumulative effect could be substantial.* ***Attractive?*** *I gave it a small 'a'. I know it is good for me to avoid fast food but, well, I do indulge on occasion.* ***Possible?*** *Absolutely.* ***Deadlined?*** *Yes – but is it the next three calendar months or the next twelve weeks starting tomorrow morning?*
7	**Love her/him madly for the rest of my life.** *This one takes us into another depth of goal setting. The objective of this book is to cover*

basics. But this is one to think about for later workbooks.

8 Make love with him/her twice a week and more on vacation – starting now!
__Measurable?__ Probably, but it might be worth establishing what constitutes 'making love' in your partner's eyes. __Attractive?__ Well in theory yes, but there might just be the possibility of a loss of spontaneity! We're getting into the more subtle elements of goal-setting here. A question for later: What would need to be happening for this goal to be attractive? __Possible?__ Well, has it worked before?
__Deadlined?__ You bet!

9 Do all the exercises in this book, with a pen, before this date: _____
Do we really need to spell this one out?

10 Forgive him/her/them from this moment on.
I put this in as a prompt for more advanced work in a later workbook.

For the moment let me say that, if understood in the context of emotional ownership, it can be a powerful and growthful goal.

11	**Loose weight by my next birthday.** *You are probably getting the hang of this by now. How much weight? Me? Loose weight? When?*
12	**Write a book by the end of next year.** *Too broad. Try the next one.*
13	**Write it to at least 250 pages and get 10 honest reviews.** *That's more like it. That's a goal.*
14	**Win the lottery and buy a house for each of my friends.** *A very small 'p'. Nice dream though!*
15	**Make a record of every time I loose my temper in the next 12 months.** ***Measurable?*** *You might like to add something like 'and write 50 words about the context'.* ***Attractive?*** *Well, for some it might have a potential positive outcome but might be hard work in and of itself.* ***Possible?*** *Why not?* ***Deadlined?*** *Seems to be.*

So there is a little exercise in goal-setting. See how different it is to dreaming? Now, try a little goal-setting.

Strategy No.6 :   Set some goals!

Start Here:

6.1. Set some little goals.

Little goal 1: _____

_____

Measured by: _____

Attractive because: _____

Possible? (yes or no): _____

Deadline: _____

Progress report: _____

_____
_____
_____
_____
_____
_____
_____

Growing Me – The Basics

Little goal 2: _____

_____

Measured by: _____

Attractive because: _____

Possible? (yes or no): _____

Deadline: _____

Progress report:_____

_____

_____

Little goal 3: _____

_____

Measured by: _____

Attractive because: _____

Possible? (yes or no): _____

Deadline: _____

Progress report:

_____

_____

_____

6.2. Set One Medium Goal.

Medium Goal: _____
_____
_____

Measured by: _____
Attractive because: _____
_____

Possible? (yes or no): _____
Deadline: _____
Progress report: _____
_____
_____
_____
_____
_____
_____
_____
_____

6.3. Set One Big Goal?
(Have you done your dreaming?)

The Big One: _____

_____

_____

Measured by: _____

Attractive because: _____

_____

Possible? (yes or no): _____

Deadline: _____

Progress report: _____

_____

_____

_____

_____

_____

_____

_____

This chapter has presented a basic approach to goal-setting. Wouldn't it be nice if life was so simple! The activity of simply applying ourselves to goal-setting begins to move us into new territory. Remember to keep your notes for later workbooks.

7. Review.

If you have worked through the book to this point you will have covered six basic ideas for meaningful living:

1. Understanding personal growth.
2. Limbering up your thinking.
3. Beginning to take emotional ownership.
4. Looking after your hardware (your body).
5. Dreaming – the basics.
6. Basic goal-setting.

This book is the first of a series of workbooks designed to be practical, straight forward and inexpensive. If you were learning a musical instrument, you would likely have to practice your scales so that you can later take on pieces of increasing complexity. These six areas, and additional subjects, will be covered in increasing depth and sophistication in subsequent workbooks. It is in the nature of personal growth that subtleties and new challenges emerge as we engage with the process. Please do not underestimate the value of starting with, or going back to, the basics. This is what solid foundations are made of and structures of substance are built upon.

Meaningful personal growth not only challenges the grower but also the people around them. Giving a copy of this workbook to a number of people close to you may support that process.

The Growing Me™ philosophy is to provide practical life tools, at an affordable price, to people who wish to build and sustain meaningful lives. If you would like any particular area covered by a future workbook in the series, or you would like more information on the Growing Me™ initiative, please visit the website: **www.growingme.com**

Growing Me – The Basics

Séamus Scanlan

Made in the USA